Heikki Huotari

TO JUSTIFY THE BUTTERFLY

SurVision Books

First published in 2023 by
SurVision Books
Dublin, Ireland
Reggio di Calabria, Italy
www.survisionmagazine.com

Copyright © Heikki Huotari, 2023

Design © SurVision Books, 2023

ISBN: 978-1-912963-41-6

This book is in copyright. No part of this publication may be reproduced, stored in a retrieval system, or transmitted in any form or by any means without the prior permission in writing from the publisher.

Acknowledgments

Grateful acknowledgment is made to the editors of the following, in which some of these poems, or versions of them, originally appeared:

Blue as an Orange Magazine: "The Empty Set 1-8"

Concision: "Freeing Zebras"

Faultline: "On Stalking the Inclusive Or"

Filling Station: "Empathy or Proprioception" and "Remote Sensing"

Fjords Review: "Ode to a Personal Boundary"

Heavy Feather Review: "Content"

The Night Heron Barks: "Esperanza 1-4"

Offcourse: "To the Data Driven," "On the Clock," and "The Crime of Calculation"

Primeval Monster: "The Doctor Not the Monster 1-4"

Rogue Agent: "Autoimmune"

CONTENTS

On the Clock	5
The Crime of Calculation	6
To the Data Driven	7
Content	8
Ode to a Personal Boundary	10
Autoimmune	11
Freeing Zebras	12
The Empty Set	13
The Doctor Not the Monster	21
Remote Sensing	25
Empathy or Proprioception	26
Esperanza	27
On Stalking the Inclusive Or	31

On the Clock

if it's not a ratio then it's not a rate of change   the pigs when greased are keeping their own counsel   does Walt Whitman contradict me   very well Walt Whitman contradicts me   there are three and one half adults in your average time machine   consider lilies but don't give the sleeping dog a second thought   the highest and the lowest scores are cut because they might be biased   have you seen the good cop and the bad cop in a room together   which of the ingredients is secret and how many purposes are served   so colorful my costume I'm a hero and I'm on the clock

The Crime of Calculation

I'll do my part and be a witness to the systematic desecration as one tendril to another tendril's tending so the crime of calculation to the anticrime of passion so my ribbon says PARTICIPANT and we participants are put on one leg at a time by put on I might mean our legs are pulled   our legs are pulled through cylinders   our legs have suction cups   I have a fragile hat to sit on and a velvet pillow to wear on my head   the debits and the words of Jesus are in red   the schools of fish have rendezvous on Tuesdays   close the door in my face will you take my blushing husband please

To the Data Driven

the elevator operator says floor please   half off the road the immune system's waving to the viral variant to go around   as of today there are two kinds of nervous systems   willows weep not just because of their poor posture   as they're carbon based my predecessors turn their pleasure makers up to ten   I tell some graduates to be obsessive and compulsive   even anecdotes are data to the data driven   extrasensory perception's wasted on the extrasensory-perceptive   one rare manuscript is handled with white gloves   I tell some tag-alongs to blame the victim   as it takes a multiple of two to tango so to rule the universe it takes a multiple of three

Content

1. should a safe be dropped then so should a piano and to music and to money both should open   I say privatize the positive and socialize the negative and call it content   here a template there a template everywhere a template   in the same way that I hope for your sake that your traffic lights are synchronized I hope for your sake that your elevator buttons aren't placebos every isolated light an urchin   between each two saints a sinner   in anticipation of a payoff Kubla Kahn would shut the definition down   then I'd say hello phone I'll be your live one then declining I'd lie on the park bench and I'd call to joggers you can do it you can grow up to be what you want

2. there's no ellipsoid without eccentricity   the marble which is not part of a torso is removed   there is a gun for every cold dead hand   my bible says that bats are birds   with energy and matter switched at birth and switched again at death all's well the cataclysm justifies the butterfly the butterfly the caterpillar vested double-breasted buoyant bullet proof agape what sin of omission are you contemplating now   anomalies are measurement mistakes whereby the expectation stands ingenious I'm setting up a road block and I vow to overlook no tourist bus   pro forma though my blandishment my blandishment is taken seriously by the kitchen god   the kitchen god says I can live with that   the aliases have been altered to protect the relatively innocent   the innocent whose excuse is that they feared for their life

3. to live by logic is to die by logic   may my window be a mirror to the preening miscreant within   through dedicated sets of repetitions preening miscreants have strong emotions   what were minor mental muscles bulge   direction vectors absently allotted paper trails are parametrically defined in perpetuity an animal in increments I'm shedding dreadful skin   what to replace my vacuum with   what social graces lurk in hearts of humanoids what dreadful politesse   the truisms of isolation are twice filtered and pursuant to an all-encompassing digression resources are pooled   not taking yes for an answer I'm having my way and I'm turning blue   a broken eight-hour clock is right three times a day   it's either phobia or choice or green fatigue if e is time and m is place and c is rate of change then for each would-be clone there is an antidote to true to   exorcised some essences are intersecting   now they're tables now they're chairs   the single data cable passes through the octopus's garden and the data are enabled   let's just say the data have their ways

Ode to a Personal Boundary

you can't stand behind the president in camo and be in the space force too   a convex combination of no atrophy no rigor mortis and no octopod you'll situate your shoes on one floor at a time   one fish reminds an ocean of another

vigilantes not yet good Samaritans no falsely prosecuted perpetrators languish on death row   you'll ask or not for whom the decibels or Richter scales   a minor fifth would be as diabolical   your boundary is exact

your one condition necessary and sufficient you'll be tested next as in the land of five-eyed flies the six-eyed fly is king what would you not wear in your hair in lieu of pleasure

bending threats into a greeting   you'll have angels at all angles now and craving later   you'll know where your entropy has been   you'll start your engines' engines gentlemen and idle   if you don't console yourselves who will

Autoimmune

the hex is bad the lack is worse and the proportions are exaggerated   when the lane is elongated by the fence my contribution to the conversation ends with I want more and when the body not of birdsong and the other body not of birdsong meet the body tripping through the morgue   when into my periphery then past my picture window flies the freewheel cartilage and sinew go to war

what slope is less than slippery   what force of darkness has the fewest least redeeming features   as adulterated venom's better either one man's half life is another's doubling time or your disintegration my solidity my designated drive to drink   I wake to wheels and wheels deceive me neatly   entropy compounding error effortlessly   there's no pareidolia except in pancakes and accepting silence I will dance at drops of hats and I will know the score

Freeing Zebras

shy of certainty you'll ask the school of fish what school of fish it is and if you act your age then Jesus will have naught to do with you   the supplement   the salt lick   will become the tongue

as past extrapolation holds no candle gawking at a flora or a fauna I become one   I can't have what the Almighty's having so I'll have what the Almighty recommends   what could go wrong

to those opposed to knowing clones I offer my anthology   to all I did or will offend   the bifurcation and postponement bifurcated and postponed will someone scramble my priorities while I'm not watching   why won't someone ask the midpoint what the difference between the two endpoints is

by dint of my detection elementary particles spin neither up nor down   there is no blood on my hands   though caught in the act of freeing zebras I deny I'm setting zebras free

The Empty Set 1

my environment my rules maintains the mayfly to the flexible ephemera   to enter my periphery be pale green tentacles in twos   the time of life   three ten a.m.   is duly noted and some soft warm animals are scurrying in furrows   furrows know the pixel by the company the pixel keeps   I need a counterweight because of course I do   because this function is continuous and here it's positive and there it's negative this function has a zero and the zero is on one side of the midpoint or the other   this with iteration may approximate the zero to whatever accuracy one may choose

The Empty Set 2

one of five finalists I'm tweaking three parameters and predator and prey become competing species   though the angles of reflection and of incidence are equal the reflecting surface is uncertainty   emerging two or more magicians miles downstream   imagine my contortion when I take to heart one admonition then another   if I indicate an object then I speak its name   fluorescent are endorphins but endorphins oriented every which way and I'm maximally comfortable on concrete then a coyote running side by side is recreation   then concatenated fractally   how indirect upon Mt Rushmore are the objects of

The Empty Set 3

affection and derision both of you   sing me a song and I'll feed turtles lettuce   there are more speeds in reverse than dreamed of in your forwardness your forwardness   my nightmares in increasing order my coincidences uncoordinated daily and in distance increments per increment of time   as everything is left to the imagination in the look of love the syllables are names for names for notes   the farmer's found a shortcut and the farmer stands alone   we have no need of necks to kneel on we have badges   no two artifacts were ever less antipodal and no remark was pointed more   two hats are passed because the second cause though just as worthy is the second third world war

The Empty Set 4

and God said May the number zero be associated with the empty set   on hearing car alarms God hardened Pharaoh's heart   on losing contact with reality I send my complements to who was terminated yesterday   the prisoner of consciousness is glancing at a landscape and the prisoner of consciousness's sanity's exact   I'd never curse an animal with ears says Goldilocks dismissing simultaneously ultraviolet and infrared   accelerometers do not fall far from trees   but three and one half adolescents in your average time machine   what next will mortals make of precedent and antecedent   strike me lightning twice and shame on me

The Empty Set 5

some thumbs say to some fingers Who's opposing who   I'm walking back my happiness at ease   I'm well advised to hold the silver chalice tentatively to extrapolate from random passages   change one of my parameters and I would be diminished   of the two competing deities how will I know which is the good one   as Magellan sails from Point A to Point A in record time   as dogs approach their beds in perfect circles so philosophy of life provides no balm no bane   a cantilever wants a counterweight   as genders are revealed so rudiments are nutrients in backwards land

The Empty Set 6

by who or what abutted where's Mount Fuji now   on the inclusion-exclusion continuum I'd have a wild ride for no more than fifteen minutes   the eyes of attorneys general are the windows of attorneys general's souls   please pass the polygraph   be Bachelor Number Three   within one standard deviation of the average hummingbird are mourning doves pretending not to be   to each an incidental mechanism   false horizon   intersection of continua   to each a color between green and blue   it's twilight time   it's choice fatigue   it's man's best friend or better   velvet rope on stainless post deny me but to guide me   I would learn caesura plurally   potential energy a mouth to feed   of zero and the empty set who's representing who

The Empty Set 7

I will not dance if there's no hat rack even with my sister even if not one of twelve apostles' blossoms please me   I will be a variant when all my proper subsets disagree   there's no use crying over separated milk   the flavor of the day is insufficient to my needs   a fingerprint with missing whorls would be as tactful as an adolescent with a learning style as rapt so may I pester you with questions   shall I haul out my all-purpose who-what-when-where-why must voices take the place of wills   the baby needs new shoes   I want a phase shift for my body clock pursuant to the rending and amending of the minutes of the meeting I'll sell my scenario   the royal they may make their way anonymously to the sons and daughters of departed tsars

The Empty Set 8

I'm trading up a hairpin for a house a geostationary satellite an Aristotle molecule and two of you to make the old joke new unchain the expectation it's a kangaroo an interval of which the endpoints are tin cans   each martyr to the scientific method has a null hypotheses to bear   appendage of no overtone I might at any minute lose a tooth   past half lives half undressed my isotope is out of touch to lunch   should you be burning furniture or undervaluing two truths that's Doctor Followup to you right angle of an arm   my interlocutor says do you want to make something of it and I say maybe later

The Doctor Not the Monster 1

the crooked stick says I know where the bodies are   expunge my record while I mix and match these heroes and these villains   think tanks run by children are the lucky ones   how many feet must centipedes have in the grave   I stop half on half off the road and wave to the impatient Go around   as in the common room I think about what has been done to me I segue from scenario to premise and I ask Who is the opposite of that masked man   is that a spotless conscience on the road ahead is that your omniverse or are you glad to see me   the sincerest form of flattery is cut and fill   but twelve more dead-sea circuits and this bed of nails is mine   when entropy's thrown for a loop my climate science is adopted   of a lifetime it's the opportunity   so throw away that rule book throw away that crutch   amygdalas are running rampant   seen not heard the young earth grins from ear to ear to ear   a mullion squares a moon up as on Mars it's seventeen a.m.   I'm throwing chairs around so later I'll feel less than loved

The Doctor Not the Monster 2

neither blot nor scribble be but patterned after   I won't say there is asymmetry but I'll live well without it   when a woman poses as a man who's posing as a woman when the astral body's astral body takes a detour it's a shortcut   at the quantum level clowns are funny only every now and then and you are just as likely laughing with as at   what time is it where you are   if you be my alibi I'll ask then act your age   unanimous as is the practice that is codified by me and architectural the oversight that I inspire each apparently incriminating statement has a context of its own

if ants or atoms my periphery is detailed and receding   window in the floor or mirror on the ceiling we're confessing even as we preen   the moral agent's take is ten percent   a magnitude and a direction and a vector et voilà there is no cardinality between those of the rationals and reals   the ways of cake are perpendicular to flights of pies   go over under or around the obstacle   get no participation prize

accelerometers are going rogue   resisting cardiac arrest behind each fig leaf there's a naughty bit and if largess is left I'll give it to the challenger and if largess is left I'll give it to the challenged and with ample media to dream in three cheerleaders throw me in the air and chant Bring out your dead your bugaboo your barbecue   I'll be as keen to please as that bomb-sniffing dog   if on the spectrum there's a gender I can't live with or without then will the curiosities that were amusing now repel or will the curiosities that were repulsive now amuse

The Doctor Not the Monster 3

stepping off a distance I might push a boat back I might burn a bridge   as from an exile exiled large is close and small is far and between stick and carrot falls the fiction   as by magic now I see three ossicles immersed in viscous labyrinths and now I don't with sins remembered sins forgiven in sequential demolition of abandoned block-long buildings   Adolph Hitler loves me Baby Jesus loves me more   what light is isolated   I identify with lemurs equally   due to my loyalty to gravity tautologies are only conversation starters   don't transition in a huff but just   parameters through sequiturs obey Hooke's Law   in lieu of furniture dismantle oxeye daisies drink from self-selected prequels   the vestigial tail that I've divested myself of is entertaining predators   my food includes all flying objects objects unidentified and non-existent   give or take a manatee permission slips are Freudian no two the same no butterfly to blame   adjacent brains are better than their neighbors   there are seven things that poets don't want you to know   click HERE

The Doctor Not the Monster 4

not your punching bag I forego body English and ecstatically roll gutter balls   my drunken alter ego's at the hop adjusting to that awesome new environment and as it takes a word to know a word your package from Alaska has arrived and I defer to those who say they're on a mission and if spots are out then stripes are in   on my watch there will be no rarefaction though I may malign the members of my family you may not my other mother and no matter what Erato says the Axiom of Choice is yours and if you like your incandescent light bulb you can keep it

halve the width of human hair or multiply the length the impulse is the same the turning of the head commences reason is impeded reason   inclusive or exclusive this migraine aura or a state-of-the-heart scarred what can I add to make the offer more attractive   twins stop bickering you're both right it's a scaffold and it's a mirage   as boys would have been boys but some more so than others time has endpoints only I sleep well

Remote Sensing

tonsils call appendices tangential   tonsils tiptoe and consider tulips tiptoed through   how adventitious is the motion of the newly nameless   venues mend their ways and dismiss minions minion's sentiments are genuine   what I bring to the table is a metaphor

I'm at the end of B Street and from fog jumps out at me a monkey puzzle tree   there are no smallest particles and no most mortal   out with obsolescence in with remote sensing nodes from vocal cords removed   is Baby Jesus bad at hide-and-seek not quite clear on the concept   Are you in the closet I ask Baby Jesus   Baby Jesus says Amen

they doubt position and velocity but not acceleration   will they laugh when I sit down to play the alpenhorn   in semi-privacy I'll circumvent no law of logic contemplate but null hypotheses and in the margin tabulate expected variation   I've got sample mean and sample standard deviation   who could ask for more

Empathy or Proprioception

equivalence classes and figures eight of speech   you think therefore I am   I think therefore you are   through rabbits (they're like rabbits) and connoting we will go   though brevity's belabored and eternity's de-emphasized more than alive I'm between breath and death   my body is a temple and

I brake for singing telegrams   at what scale does this room not loom   why did the demon cross the street   three bobbleheads their eyes wide positively charged emit advice   be struck by lightning neither twice in one place nor in two locations at one time   appearances your hearts and minds be neither vertically or horizontally aligned   if you sit through the second feature maybe then you'll get your money's worth

Esperanza 1

bring on board the expectation   as electric circuit is to spring-mass-damper so prepared remark to from-the-heart   the negative of face-to-face a vase   the moving sidewalk doesn't end but your connection does   when relegated to miscellany your knowledge of position and your knowledge of velocity may simultaneously fade   it's good to stop and smell the rotting carcass but it's better yet to roll in it and take your essence with you to the ozone   an air-pressure differential will cause doors to open on their own

Esperanza 2

the houses as time passes migrate with the climate   not one christian soldier marches as to war   as oscillations not orthogonal are micromanaged so I'll have a hive mind don't mind if I do   I'll be so full of grace my books will balance on their own   my students will have social skills   as misdirected as is expectation mountain dwellers crave confinement   as the content may have shifted so the consolation   may I find the prize like Einstein   may I drive the speed of light from information to misinformation   may my moving sidewalk never end

Esperanza 3

blesséd are the shivering for they'll be blanketed commemorated   one leg short the water table wobbles   take your grievance and your gratitude outside   the opaque is the enemy of the translucent   if Narcissus manifests with bits of wisdom insulating my surround the indistinguishable faces of a tetrahedron bring to me my volatile organic compound   it's a crystal   every day is prestidigitation day   the probability of partly sunny is the probability of partly cloudy and the novel by analogy is known

Esperanza 4

consistent with the trivial equivalence   for every x and every y x and y are related   when the demonstrators let their limbs go limp the police wave their sticks   if walking is not falling so is flying   when blood rushes to my head my spine aligns with gravity in but one of two ways   she loves me and she loves my dog or not   try what the climate migrants try   an harp said Ezra Pound ironically upending an erosion an inclusive or   don't put the fire out till you see the dark parts of their eyes   it's always all about the living thing

On Stalking the Inclusive Or

from butterfly to otherwise I'm speaking not in tongues but blaming snakes   I live beside the spectrum and befriend   of business going out or for the eyes of two or more potatoes are upon you or your patriot is killed by friendly fire

the self-involved are swearing independent oaths   to have and hold or have not hold or hold not have or neither have nor hold or you may make the most of two or three degrees of freedom or you're laughing on the outside/crying on the inside or you're crying on the outside/laughing on the inside or it's with the dull knife that you cut yourself or to the hammer every problem is a nail

Erato says you're making sense again   the centipede and centrifuge are waiting for the other shoe to fall   your gargoyle acts as if your other gargoyle hasn't seen it all

Selected Poetry Titles Published by SurVision Books

Seeds of Gravity: An Anthology of Contemporary Surrealist Poetry from Ireland
 Edited by Anatoly Kudryavitsky
 ISBN 978-1-912963-18-8

Invasion: An Anthology of Ukrainian Poetry about the War
 Edited by Tony Kitt
 ISBN 978-1-912963-32-4

Noelle Kocot. *Humanity*
 (New Poetics: USA)
 ISBN 978-1-9995903-0-7

Marc Vincenz. *Einstein Fledermaus*
 (New Poetics: USA)
 ISBN 978-1-912963-20-1

Helen Ivory. *Maps of the Abandoned City*
 (New Poetics: England)
 ISBN 978-1-912963-04-1

Tony Kitt. *The Magic Phlute*
 (New Poetics: Ireland)
 ISBN 978-1-912963-08-9

Clayre Benzadón. *Liminal Zenith*
 (New Poetics: USA)
 ISBN 978-1-912963-11-9

Thomas Townsley. *Tangent of Ardency*
 (New Poetics: USA)
 ISBN 978-1-912963-15-7

Anton Yakovlev. *Chronos Dines Alone*
  (Winner of James Tate Poetry Prize 2018)
  ISBN 978-1-912963-01-0

Mikko Harvey & Jake Bauer. *Idaho Falls*
  (Winner of James Tate Poetry Prize 2018)
  ISBN 978-1-912963-02-7

John Bradley. *Spontaneous Mummification*
  (Winner of James Tate Poetry Prize 2019)
  ISBN 978-1-912963-13-3

John Thomas Allen. *Rolling in the Third Eye*
  (Winner of James Tate Poetry Prize 2019)
  ISBN 978-1-912963-15-7

Gary Glauber. *The Covalence of Equanimity*
  (Winner of James Tate Poetry Prize 2019)
  ISBN 978-1-912963-12-6

Charles Kell. *Pierre Mask*
  (Winner of James Tate Poetry Prize 2019)
  ISBN 978-1-912963-19-5

Charles Borkhuis. *Spontaneous Combustion*
  (Winner of James Tate Poetry Prize 2021)
  ISBN 978-1-912963-30-0

Noah Falck & Matt McBride. *Prerecorded Weather*
  (Winner of James Tate Poetry Prize 2022)
  ISBN 978-1-912963-39-3

Michael Zeferino Spring. *Kahlo's Window*
  (Winner of James Tate Poetry Prize 2022)
  ISBN 978-1-912963-40-9

George Kalamaras. *That Moment of Wept*
ISBN 978-1-9995903-7-6

George Kalamaras. *Through the Silk-Heavy Rains*
ISBN 978-1-912963-28-7

Ciaran O'Driscoll. *Angel Hour*
ISBN 978-1-912963-27-0

Oz Hardwick. *A Census of Preconceptions*
ISBN 978-1-912963-38-6

Tim Murphy. *Mouth of Shadows*
ISBN 978-1-912963-29-4

Order our books from http://survisionmagazine.com/bookshop.htm

www.ingramcontent.com/pod-product-compliance
Lightning Source LLC
Chambersburg PA
CBHW061314040426
42444CB00010B/2636